EDGE
BOOKS™

LIFE ON THE
FRONT LINES

# WORLD WAR II
## ON THE FRONT LINES

by Tim Cooke

CAPSTONE PRESS
a capstone imprint

Edge Books are published by Capstone Press,
1710 Roe Crest Drive, North Mankato, Minnesota 56003
www.capstonepub.com


Published in 2014 by Capstone Publishers, Ltd.

*Library of Congress Cataloging-in-Publication Data*

Cooke, Tim, 1961-
World War II on the front lines / by Tim Cooke.
   pages cm. -- (Edge books. Life on the front lines)
Summary: "Approaches the topic of World War II from the perspective
of those fighting in it"-- Provided by publisher.
 ISBN 978-1-4914-0844-5 (library binding) -- ISBN 978-1-4914-0850-6
 (pbk.)
1. World War, 1939-1945--Juvenile literature. 2. World War,
1939-1945--Social aspects--Juvenile literature. 3. Soldiers--United
States--History--20th century--Juvenile literature. I. Title.

D743.7.C674 2014
940.54'1273--dc23

                    2014001506

For Brown Bear Books Ltd:
Editorial Director: Lindsey Lowe
Text: Tim Cooke
Children's Publisher: Anne O'Daly
Design Manager: Keith Davis
Designer: Lynne Lennon
Picture Manager: Sophie Mortimer
Production Director: Alastair Gourlay

**Source Notes**
**p.9** Robert F. Gallagher, from "Scratch One Messerscmitt," http://www.gallagher.com/ww2/chapter2.html; **p.11** Corporal at Camp
Book, from http://wwiiletters.blogspot.co.uk/2009/02/camp-cooke-california-wwii-letter.html; **p.13** Robert F. Gallagher, from http://
www.gallagher.com/ww2/chapter11.html; **p.17** Deane E. Marks, from "No One Smiled on Leyte," http://www.thedropzone.org/
pacific/marks2.htm; **p.19** soldier in the Pacific, quoted in *The U.S. Army In World War II* by Mark R. Henry, Osprey Publishing,
2001, p.24; **p.21** Esther Edwards, from Battle of the Bulge, WGBH American Experience, PBS, http://www.pbs.org/wgbh/
americanexperience/features/primary-resources/bulge-nurse/; **p.23** Robert Edlin, from http://www.eyewitnesstohistory.com/dday2.
htm; **p.27** Ernest Uno, quoted from *War Letters: Extraordinary Correspondence from American Wars* by Andrew Carroll, Simon & Schuster,
2002, p225; **p.29** Keith Winston, from *V-Mail. Letters of a World War II Combat Medic* by Keith Winston, Algonquin Books of Chapel
Hill, 1985, p.40.

**Photo Credits**
**Front Cover**: Robert Hunt Library
**All interior images:** Robert Hunt Library except Getty Images: New York Daily News 9b, Popperfoto 19br, Ralph Morse/Time & Life
Pictures 25; National Archives and Records Administration: 7, 10, 18, 21tl, 21br, 26, 27br, 28, 29tr; U.S. Army Signal Corps 17t;
U.S. Army Airforce 24;
**Artistic effects:** Shutterstock

# TABLE OF CONTENTS

# WORLD WAR II

World War II (1939–1945) began in Europe in September 1939, when Nazi Germany, led by Adolf Hitler, invaded Poland. Great Britain and France declared war on Germany. Germany invaded much of northwest and central Europe. By late 1940, Japan had joined with Germany and its ally, Italy. They were known as the **Axis powers**. In June 1941, Germany invaded the Soviet Union.

The United States remained neutral until December 8, 1941, one day after Japan attacked the U.S. base at Pearl Harbor in Hawaii. The United States declared war on Japan. Japan's allies, Germany and Italy, declared war on the United States.

U.S. troops wade ashore on Utah Beach on D-Day, June 6, 1944, when the Allies invaded northwest Europe.

This U.S. Army poster encouraged anyone already in the military to transfer to the infantry.

ALL SOLDIERS can't be in the INFANTRY—but

Soldiers in the United States, between the ages of 18 and 32, may apply for transfer to the Infantry. This privilege is provided by War Department Circulars 262 and 278, 1944. Ask your Commanding Officer.

U.S. forces joined British soldiers fighting the Italians and Germans in North Africa. They then captured the island of Sicily and landed in Italy. On June 6, 1944, D-Day, the **Allies** made a huge landing in Normandy, France. From there, they fought their way across northern Europe to Germany. The Germans eventually surrendered in May 1945.

In the Pacific, U.S. forces defeated the Japanese navy at Midway in June 1942. They then began to capture Japanese-held islands. After the dropping of two atomic bombs on the Japanese cities of Hiroshima and Nagasaki in August 1945, Japan surrendered.

- **Axis powers:** the term used in World War II for Germany, Italy, Japan, and the countries that fought on their side against the Allies

- **Allies:** the term used in World War II for Great Britain, the United States, the Soviet Union, and the countries that fought on their side against the Axis powers

# CHAPTER 1

# THE MAKING OF A SOLDIER

At the start of World War II in Europe in 1939, the United States military was in no shape to join the fight. The Army had fewer than 200,000 soldiers, and its weapons were out of date. Soldiers still wore World War I (1914–1918) helmets. But the United States wanted to be prepared in case it did need to join the fight. The U.S. government conducted large-scale recruitment efforts and made a huge investment in new equipment.

U.S. soldiers in training carry out a simulated attack as smoke bombs go off around them.

After the Japanese attack on Pearl Harbor on December 7, 1941, the possibility of going to war became a reality. The previous year a **draft** had been started. It forced men between the ages of 21 and 36 to sign up for 12 months. By the time of the Pearl Harbor attack, the U.S. military had grown to 2.2 million soldiers, sailors, airmen, and Marines. Most of the new recruits were draftees. Eventually, 10 million men were drafted into military service.

The African-American 41st Engineers parade at Fort Bragg in 1942 to mark the completion of their training.

• **draft:** a system of selecting men for compulsory service in the army

# RECRUITMENT AND THE DRAFT

Recruiting soldiers was the job of 6,443 draft boards across the country. The board members judged each man on his health, his family situation, and the importance of his job at home. Suitable recruits were put into a drawing and their numbers were pulled out until the draft was full. Men often volunteered instead of waiting to be drafted. That way they could choose which branch of the military to join. Recruiting posters were put up everywhere.

The most famous recruiting poster featured Uncle Sam. It appealed to the nation's sense of patriotism.

This recruiting poster displays the shoulder badges that men could get if they were promoted to higher ranks.

## EYEWITNESS

NAME: Robert F. Gallagher
UNIT: U.S. 815th Anti-Aircraft Artillery
Battalion, 3rd Army

"Knowing that I was finally going was more a relief than anything else. I had been ready for a long time, and the act of doing it just seemed routine. Routine! There would be nothing routine about what I was about to experience for the better part of the next three years of my life."

New recruits were given health checks before joining the regular U.S. Army.

# TRAINING

New recruits had to be trained to be soldiers. Training camps were set up across the country. They had rows and rows of wooden huts. Each camp housed as many as 80,000 men. Army regulars trained the new recruits. Recruits got physically fit and learned to operate and maintain their weapons. They also learned to follow orders and how to march in time.

The amount of time a recruit spent in basic training varied between **battalions**. Some men trained for 18 weeks, some for longer. After basic training some men were chosen to learn special skills.

Men of Company F of the 347th Infantry Regiment lay out their gear for inspection in a training camp in Tennessee in 1943.

U.S. soldiers who have just arrived in Europe by ship from America do exercises on the side of the dock.

Recruits tackle the assault course at Camp Edwards, Massachusetts.

• **battalion:** a large group of soldiers prepared for battle, usually an infantry unit that is part of a brigade

# TRANSPORTATION

There was only one way to get millions of troops across the globe, and that was by ship. Trains took soldiers from their training camps to ports in New York and California to travel to Europe or bases in the Pacific. More than 2,700 **Liberty ships** were built to transport troops and equipment. Luxury ocean liners were also used as troop carriers. Once troops were in position, they traveled by jeeps and tanks if possible. More often than not, however, they relied on their own two feet to get around.

U.S. troops hitch a ride on an M10 tank destroyer at the end of the war in Europe.

U.S. soldiers use rope ladders to leave their ship in North Africa in November 1942.

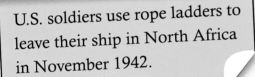

German prisoners are shipped to captivity in Britain after D-Day.

• **Liberty ship:** a cargo ship built quickly and cheaply to a standard plan in U.S. shipyards in order to support the war effort

13

# CHAPTER 2

# AT THE FRONT

Life on the front lines varied depending on whether soldiers were in Europe, North Africa, or the Pacific region. In Europe soldiers faced cold winters. During the Battle of the Bulge on the French border in 1945, the wounded froze to death. In North Africa, the desert sun caused sunstroke and sunburn. On Pacific islands, the heat and monsoon rain made life difficult. Disease was common, and there were poisonous snakes and insects.

U.S. Marines come under Japanese fire on Okinawa in the Pacific in April 1945.

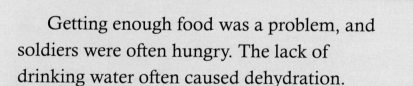

Getting enough food was a problem, and soldiers were often hungry. The lack of drinking water often caused dehydration.

Under such difficult conditions, a strong sense of comradeship was all that kept soldiers' spirits up. Allied soldiers shared a strong belief that they were fighting to rid the world of **fascism** and **militarism**. Their enemies were eager to spread their own beliefs around the world.

A U.S. infantryman lying down on a road in France uses his helmet in the hope of getting German soldiers to fire so he can figure out their location.

- **fascism:** the anti-democratic beliefs of the Nazis in Germany and the Fascists in Italy

- **militarism:** the belief that a government should use military force to gain power and achieve its goals

15

# LIVING CONDITIONS

At the front, U.S. troops slept where they could. Most soldiers slept in canvas tents. If they had no time to put up tents, they dug a **trench** and slept in the open air with just a bedroll to lie on. In North Africa, where fine sand made it difficult to dig trenches, some men slept in or under their vehicles. In the Pacific, sleeping on palm leaves spread out on the ground was common.

These tents make up the base that U.S. engineers set up near the airstrip on the island of Pelelieu in the western Pacific.

These U.S. troops used wood and palm leaves to build a shelter on Tarawa, an island in the Pacific.

A U.S. soldier relaxes in his hammock on a transport ship sailing near Iceland.

## EYEWITNESS

NAME: Deane E. Marks
UNIT: U.S. 115th Parachute Infantry Regiment

"When dusk approached, we generally would halt and start to dig in. The more time you spent digging, the more secure you felt when it started to get dark."

● **trench:** a deep, narrow ditch dug into the ground for shelter

# FOOD AND DRINK

Soldiers at the front were often hungry. They received **rations** labeled with letters to show the size of the rations. C-rations had three canned meals: stew, hash, and pork and beans. D-rations included a chocolate bar that was nicknamed "Hitler's secret weapon" because it sometimes gave soldiers stomachaches. K-rations were introduced in 1943 as smaller rations that soldiers could carry. Special jungle rations in the Pacific included Spam, dried fruits, peanuts, crackers, and candy. These rations were unpopular with soldiers. They often ate their candy and dumped the rest.

African-American U.S. military members enjoy a rare hot meal on the Aleutian Islands in May 1943.

U.S. soldiers in the Pacific improvise a stove for roasting peanuts.

U.S. troops on the front line in Belgium receive a hot meal during the winter of 1945.

● **ration:** a soldier's daily share of food

# MEDICINE AND HEALTH

In World War I just 4 out of every 100 wounded men survived. In World War II the figure rose to 50 in 100. One reason for the improvement was the new drug penicillin, which kept wounds from becoming infected. A technique called triage involved prioritizing care for the wounded soldiers most likely to survive. In the Pacific, men had medicines to prevent killer diseases such as malaria. Camps were sprayed to kill the mosquitos that caused the infection.

Supplies of blood arrive in Normandy after the D-Day landings. Blood transfusions saved the lives of many soldiers.

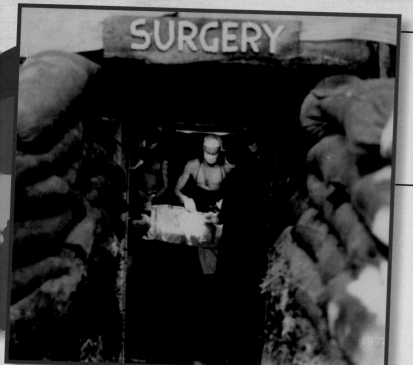

SURGERY

In an underground bunker behind the front lines, a U.S. Army doctor operates on a wounded soldier.

U.S. medics help a wounded soldier in France in 1944.

**EYEWITNESS**

NAME: Esther Edwards
POSITION: U.S. Army nurse
PLACE: Battle of the Bulge

" Patients came by ambulance and helicopter all day and night. It was overwhelming. When I tried to rest, I couldn't sleep, thinking of all those wounded patients and all that needed to be done for them. "

# UNDER FIRE

U.S. military members came under terrifying enemy fire in many instances. U.S. soldiers landing at Omaha Beach in Normandy on D-Day struggled to get ashore in the face of enemy fire. In the Pacific, U.S. Marines faced a similar nightmare when they landed on the island of Iwo Jima in 1945. More than 2,400 Marines died on the first day of the battle. Naval personnel in the Pacific also faced the threat of kamikazes. These Japanese pilots deliberately flew aircraft loaded with explosives into U.S. vessels, even though the pilots knew they were certain to be killed.

A U.S. soldier takes aim with his Springfield rifle in France after the D-Day landings.

U.S. Marines are pinned down by heavy Japanese fire as they land on the Pacific island of Peleliu.

U.S. infantrymen look anxiously from their landing craft as they approach Omaha Beach on D-Day.

● **Purple Heart:** a medal awarded to U.S. soldiers wounded or killed in action

# CHAPTER 3

# SPIRIT AND MORALE

Far from home, soldiers' emotions moved between terror and boredom. In World War I the U.S. government had learned the need to keep the spirits of the troops positive. The War Department created the Special Services department to look after troop **morale** and welfare. It sent entertainers to raise the soldiers' spirits, including stars from back home such as Glenn Miller and his orchestra.

Glenn Miller and his orchestra entertain personnel at an Allied airbase in 1944.

In U.S. training camps, baseball games, dances, and church services helped create a sense of comradeship among recruits. Closely bound units of comrades fought better when they had to face action together.

Overseas, comforts were often missing. In the Pacific the nearest recreation center might be hundreds of miles away. Only small luxuries were available, such as packs of gum. In Europe the soldiers had more chances to relax. There were clubs for servicemen and entertainment to be found in cities such as Paris, France, and London, England.

A wounded U.S. serviceman passes time in his bunk by reading a magazine.

● **morale:** the the fighting spirit of a person or group, and how confident they feel of winning a victory

# LETTERS AND BOOKS

A soldier's lifeline to home was the mail. All letters were censored to remove details the enemy might find helpful. Receiving mail from home was the highlight of many soldiers' days. Letters also arrived from people in clubs, schools, and churches, who wrote to soldiers to help keep up morale. Soldiers often read newspapers to follow events in other war zones. Many soldiers carried their own Bibles, prayer books, and other religious materials.

Soldiers visit a mobile library to choose books and magazines to read.

Sailors on a U.S. submarine are pleased to receive their mail from home.

An African-American soldier reads his Bible the night before a big U.S. attack on Manila, Philippines.

## EYEWITNESS

NAME: Ernesto Uno
UNIT: U.S. 442nd Regimental Combat Team
PLACE: Europe (writing a letter home)

" Dearest Mae,
I promised you I'd write every chance I had so here I am again. In the lull, between firing, I've found that scribbling off a few lines of a letter was the best way to ease the tension of fighting ... "

# RECREATION

In early 1941 President Franklin D. Roosevelt started the United Service Organizations (USO) to provide "a home away from home" for military personnel. By 1944 there were 3,000 USO facilities at home and abroad. At these places, soldiers could watch games, attend dances, and play games. The USO also put on shows featuring popular entertainers and movie stars. Soldiers on leave in Europe got to explore cities such as London. Those in the Pacific often headed to Australia.

Movie star and comedian Mickey Rooney entertains U.S. troops in Europe in 1945.

A priest leads a religious service on a Pacific island. Many soldiers found comfort in their spiritual beliefs.

Infantrymen in the Pacific wear plastic coats as they watch a movie outdoors in a rain storm.

## EYEWITNESS

NAME: Keith Winston
RANK: Private, 10th Infantry
PLACE: Camp Blandy, Florida

───────────────

❝ I took a walk around and ended up here in the Service Club—a beautiful place with a balcony where the boys can write letters. Downstairs is a lounging room, cafeteria, exchange, etc. ❞

# GLOSSARY

**Allies** (AL-lyz)—a group of countries that fought together in World War II; some of the Allies were the United States, Canada, Great Britain, and France

**artillery** (ar-TIL-uh-ree)—big guns such as cannons

**Axis powers** (AX-is POU-urs)—the term used in World War II for Germany, Italy, Japan, and the countries that fought on their side against the Allies

**battalion** (buh-TAL-yuhn)—a large group of soldiers prepared for battle, usually an infantry unit that is part of a brigade

**dehydration** (dee-hy-DRAY-shuhn)—when the body does not have enough water

**draft** (DRAFT)—a system of selecting men for compulsory service in the army

**fascism** (FASH--iz-uhm)—the militaristic, anti-democratic beliefs of the Nazis in Germany and the Fascists in Italy

**Liberty ship** (LIB-ur-tee SHIP)—a cargo ship built quickly and cheaply to a standard plan in U.S. shipyards in order to support the war effort

**militarism** (MIL-ut-ur-ism)—the belief that a government should use military force to gain power and achieve its goals

**monsoon** (mon-SOON)—the rainy season in parts of the Pacific

**morale** (muh-RAL)—the fighting spirit of a person or group, and how confident they feel of winning a victory

**Purple Heart** (PER-puhl HART)—a medal awarded to U.S. soldiers wounded or killed in action

**ration** (RASH-uhn)—a soldier's daily share of food

**trench** (TRENCH)—a deep, narrow ditch dug into the ground for shelter

# READ MORE

**Hamen, Susan E.** *World War II.* Essential Library of American Wars. Minneapolis: Abdo Publishing Company, 2013.

**Hamilton, John, and Sue Hamilton.** *The Final Years.* World War II. Minneapolis: Abdo Publishing Company, 2011.

**Langley, Andrew.** *World War II.* Living Through. Chicago: Heinemann-Raintree, 2012.

**Otfinoski, Steven.** *World War II Infantrymen: An Interactive History Adventure.* You Choose. North Mankato, MN: Capstone Press, 2013.

**Samuels, Charlie.** *Timeline of World War II: Europe and North Africa.* Americans at War. New York: Gareth Stevens Publishing, 2012.

**Samuels, Charlie.** *Timeline of World War II: Pacific.* Americans at War. New York: Gareth Stevens Publishing, 2012.

# INTERNET SITES

FactHound offers a safe, fun way to find Internet sites related to this book. All of the sites on FactHound have been researched by our staff.

Here's all you do:

Visit *www.facthound.com*

Type in this code: 9781491408445

Super-cool stuff!

Check out projects, games and lots more at
**www.capstonekids.com**

# INDEX